What Animal is That?

What Animal is That?

Kenneth Allen

octopus

Contents

First published in 1978 by
Octopus Books Limited
59 Grosvenor Street
London W1

ISBN 0 7064 0736 9

© 1978 Octopus Books Limited

Produced by Mandarin Publishers Limited
22a Westlands Road, Quarry Bay, Hong Kong

Printed in Singapore

endpapers: butterfly fish golden butterfly
fish and electric-blue damsel fish
half title: Pinzgauer horse from Austria
title spread: bobcat
contents: baby brown hare (leveret)

Introduction

HOW IT ALL BEGAN

Long, long ago – no one will ever really know how long – the earth we live on was a very hot ball of gas turning in the vast emptiness of space. Slowly, very slowly, it began to cool until it finally hung, a very warm, empty sphere, with hot, bubbling rivers flowing between still-steaming mountains. Many scientists agree that this was about 3,000 million years ago. Others suggest even longer.

This cooling went on until the earth began to take on a shape that was, however, nothing like we know today. It had become a jumble of hills and valleys with a surrounding atmosphere that was filled with gas and shrouded in heavy clouds. The shape of the earth was constantly changing – volcanoes and other such factors saw to that. Then the rains came, cooling down the still warm globe, filling the valleys with water which, in time, became oceans.

For another very long time there was no life whatsoever on this planet. Then, at last, a form of life arrived – no one knows how. It began in the sea and for another enormous period of time strange shapeless creatures floated on the surface of the water. On the sea beds below, green plants began to grow, making possible the animal life of later years. In time the strange floating creatures became larger, taking on definite shapes. It was during this period that jellyfish and worms first appeared.

Much later the first animals with a backbone (vertebrates, as they are called) arrived. Some of these water creatures, many now covered with scales, began to move from place to place, using a kind of swimming motion, and soon the seas began to be filled with these first, odd-looking fishes. Because of their numbers, some of these early fishes decided to see what life was like on land. Some had grown a form of legs which helped them crawl from the water onto the shore. Until this time they had breathed with their gills. They could survive in the air because they had air bladders that could be used as we use our lungs. Creatures that are able to do this – to live under water as well as on land – are called amphibians. The frog we know today is a good example of this type of creature.

By going ashore, these early creatures were following the example set by many water plants which had come onto dry land far earlier. At first these plants made their homes on mudbanks and sandy shores, letting the tides flow over them twice a day. Then, as the centuries continued to roll past, these plants began to seed further inland. And the animals coming out of the sea had to follow, for they needed these plants for food.

Some of the plants grew larger, becoming trees which made a home for the flying reptiles, some of which were the ancestors of the birds we know today. One group had membrane covered wings rather like modern bats, and they launched themselves from high cliffs or trees with a gliding flight, floating on air currents. Some, like **pteranodon,** had a wing span

of 8 metres, but others, like **pterodactylus** were no bigger than sparrows. Their long names are formed from Greek words which describe the animals – for instance, pterodactylus means an animal with a wing – pteron – supported by fingers – daktylos. Modern birds developed from a group of reptiles related to the pterosaurs. They ran upright on their back legs: over thousands of years their front legs became wings, and scales became feathers. They learned to run fast, hopping into the air, and to glide from trees. The lizard-like teeth were replaced by a beak-like mouth. **Archaeopteryx,** about the size of a crow, was half-bird, half-reptile, with feathers on its wings and long tail, but also with claws on its wings, teeth, and a long lizard-like body.

The **malleo,** a modern bird, gives us some idea of how these earlier birds must have behaved. Like modern reptiles – and the ancestors of birds – they lay their eggs in a hole scooped in the sand, cover them, and leave them to hatch on their own.

By now you must be asking how we know all about these things for, after all, they happened hundreds of millions of years ago. This is because the remains of animals and plants are still to be dug up or found in rocks. These are known as 'fossils', a word that comes from a Latin word meaning 'to dig'. The animal or plant would die, be covered by mud or sand, and this covering would change into hard rock over the centuries.

It is the 'stories' told by such fossils that have helped scientists to learn about life on this planet for millions of years.

Naturally, fossils take several forms. Sometimes the animal's bones are found. Sometimes the animal has decayed but has left an impression – a kind of mould – so that in later years the shape may still be seen. From such studies we know, for example, how big and how fierce these ancient animals were. We know, too, that

coal has come from the remains of once living plants and that chalk (or limestone) was once the shells of millions of tiny sea animals.

Even stranger things have been discovered. The fossils of sea animals high up in the Himalayas, the Rockies and the Alps prove that these great mountains were once actually under the sea!

This came about because all this time the shape of the earth was constantly changing, huge mountains crumbling and toppling into the sea whilst the sea bed would be pushed up so that it became, in time, dry land and even mountains in turn. But there came a time, as we have said, when the first plants and then animal-like lizards came ashore to take over what had been so roughly formed.

The most common of the early reptiles was a fairly small, clumsy creature called the **cotylosaur.** This is a name you have probably never heard, but he was one of the most important little fellows that ever lived. Dinosaurs became his descendants, but they are now all dead. What is far more important is that today's reptiles, birds and even mammals – and that includes us – can be traced back to him. This tracing really begins with some of the cotylosaur's descendants, the **thecodonts,** the true great-grandfather of the great dinosaurs.

During all this time the earth itself was still slowly changing. It became filled with great forests, especially huge tree ferns and conifers, and these forests, the plains and the seashore soon began to be filled with those amazing creatures of the past – the dinosaurs. This word comes from the Greek; *deinos* meaning terrible and *sauros* meaning lizard. And terrible lizards many of them were, too.

The fiercest of all these dinosaurs was one with a long and rather frightening name of **tyrannosaurus rex,** meaning, the King of the Tyrants. Huge and scaly, walking erect on its huge hind feet, it was the true king of the dinosaurs. Almost no creature of the time was safe from its great, gaping jaws and its rows of sword-like teeth.

Probably the ugliest of all these early, animals, was the **triceratops.** He gained this name because he had three horns ('tri' meaning three). Two huge horns were on his head, another stuck out of his snout. Yet for the most part he lived mainly on plants, his horns and teeth were merely to defend himself.

Curiously, the largest of these dinosaurs were all 'vegetarians', living only on plants and foliage. The one which is thought to have been the biggest that ever lumbered across the earth was the **brachiosaurus,** and that really was big! Think of the largest elephant you have ever seen, then try and imagine a creature at least 10 times as heavy. It often weighed far more than 50 tonnes.

Two other plant eaters were the **brontosaurus,** 21m (70 feet) long and weighing about 35 tonnes and its 'cousin', the **diplodocus,** which was up to 26m

(87 feet) long. The dinosaurs were constantly dying off and being replaced by other quite different types, for about 100 million years, and finally died out altogether.

Once the dinosaurs began to disappear, the mammals began to move out of their hiding places in the forests and deep undergrowth. In time they were to take over the world. They had a great advantage. The world was slowly growing cooler, and they had warm blood and hairy coats to protect them. Also, they did not lay eggs which needed the warmth of the sun to hatch them, as did the reptiles.

The earliest mammals were small creatures, some no larger than a mouse. But they soon began to grow until many were similar to the **rhinoceros,** but even

larger. All these early mammals were to become the ancestors of the animals we know today.

The first horse was the **hyracotherium,** or **eohippus,** an animal the size of a large dog, with a small head and short neck. It first existed in North America, slowly became like the horse we know today, then disappeared from there. There were none in the whole of the great continent until some were brought in again by the Spaniards in the early 16th century. By then, however, horses had spread into Europe and Asia.

In those early days of the mammals, many proved almost as terrible as the dinosaurs they had displaced. One was the **sabre-toothed tiger,** and there were other similar wild cats. But a new kind of animal had arrived. It was called a primate. It was the first animal to have its eyes set in the front of its head rather than the side and which used its front feet as hands instead of paws. But what was even more important, it had a much larger brain than the rest which allowed it to use its eyes, hands and brain together. From these primates, finally came man.

He had many enemies to face. One of these was the **mammoth.** It lived in Asia, Europe and Alaska, and had a thick, furry coat. This coat was to prove very useful, for what was to become known as the Ice Age was on its way. Masses of ice began to form all over the northern parts of the world, terrible, deep layers of ice. In Norway, for example, this ice was more than 1,800m (6,000 feet) deep in places; large parts of Britain were also covered by

the same great layers of ice which stretched, without a break, to the Scandinavian countries. The terrible cold of the Ice Age soon killed off many of the animals which had managed to survive from ancient times. For the most part, only those who had the right kind of furry protection or who had brains to seek shelter in caves and elsewhere escaped being frozen to death.

Amongst the animals suffering in this way was the latest of the primates – early man – the ancient cave dweller of the Old Stone Age. This was the time following the great Ice Age. He grew to be clever, hunting animals for food although he often had to protect himself, for he had to fight the mammoth, whose great curved tusks could tear him apart, the hairy rhinoceros; the cave bear and others, all equally frightening. But he survived; they did not. Slowly he found himself surrounded by the kind of animals that were more or less like those we know today.

Stone Age or neanderthal man lived in tribes, some of which developed more elaborate skills and tools. This was cro-magnon man, who was able to walk erect, not shuffling along like an ape. He became our ancestor, and neanderthal man slowly disappeared.

As the Ice Age passed away, the world, as we know it, really began. Early man apart, it was full of all kinds of fascinating animals; some very large, some very tiny; some pretty, some ugly. But all very interesting. Most of these, despite man, are still alive today and it is of many of them that this book is all about.

Next time you see a picture of an animal, or visit a zoo you will not ask – 'What animal is that?' . . . you will know!

Life in the seas

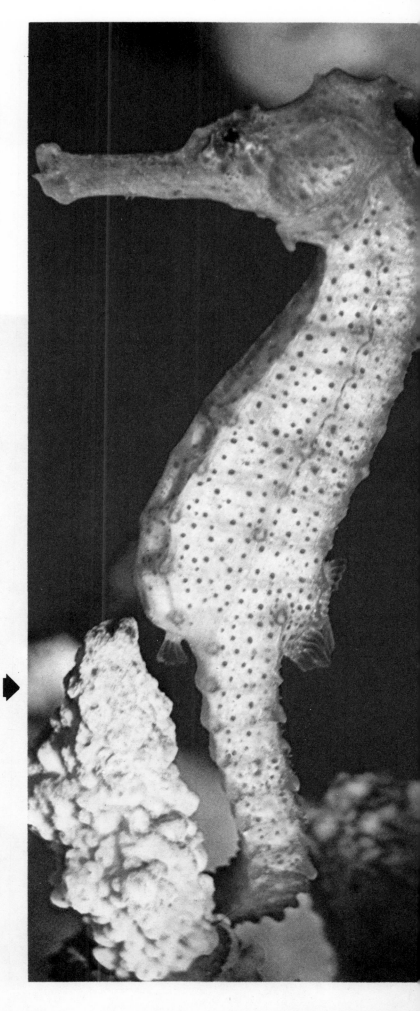

All land life, it is known, came from the sea. Yet as our oceans and seas cover nearly three-quarters of our globe, there are still plenty of fish in the sea. No one, of course, knows how many. Indeed, new types of fish and ocean life are constantly being found. Let us look at some of the most interesting.

◀ CLAM

One of the oldest sea dwellers, the **clams,** filter minute creatures for food, closing their shells tight when in danger. They are found in many oceans but the most amazing of all, however, are those found living in the crevices of the Great Barrier Reef of Australia. Rightly known as 'giant' clams, some grow to nearly 1.5m (five feet) in length. They are usually found in lagoons and reef flats and have been known to trap a diver by his foot.

SEA-HORSE

This is one of the strange sea creatures usually found in tropical waters. One variety lives in the Mediterranean and sometimes visits Britain. Its name comes from the way in which the head, somewhat horse-shaped, is placed on its trunk. It is a very poor swimmer and allows itself to be carried along by wind and waves, often clinging to floating seaweed. It is unusual because the male has a pouch on the front of its body into which the female presses her eggs. From then on the father **sea-horse** looks after them until the babies appear.

DEEP SEA FISH

Off Mindanao in the Philippines, the ocean is 10,800m (35,400 feet) deep – and that is nearly 11km (7 miles)! No one really knows all the strange creatures that live there. The pressure of water at such depths is enormous and if the fishes are brought up too quickly . . . they burst! The **stareaters** live at a depth of about 700m (2,300 feet), having a lure on the lower jaw with which they attract the creatures they feed on.

SCORPION FISH

A prick from this poisonous fish is always very painful, but seldom fatal. Many swimmers have found to their cost that as soon as they are pricked, they feel a pain which becomes so terrible that they soon become unconscious. If rushed to hospital at once there is a chance of recovery but months of treatment are needed.
Scorpion fish are usually found on rocky areas of sea-floor in the Mediterranean and in the Atlantic as far north as Biscay.

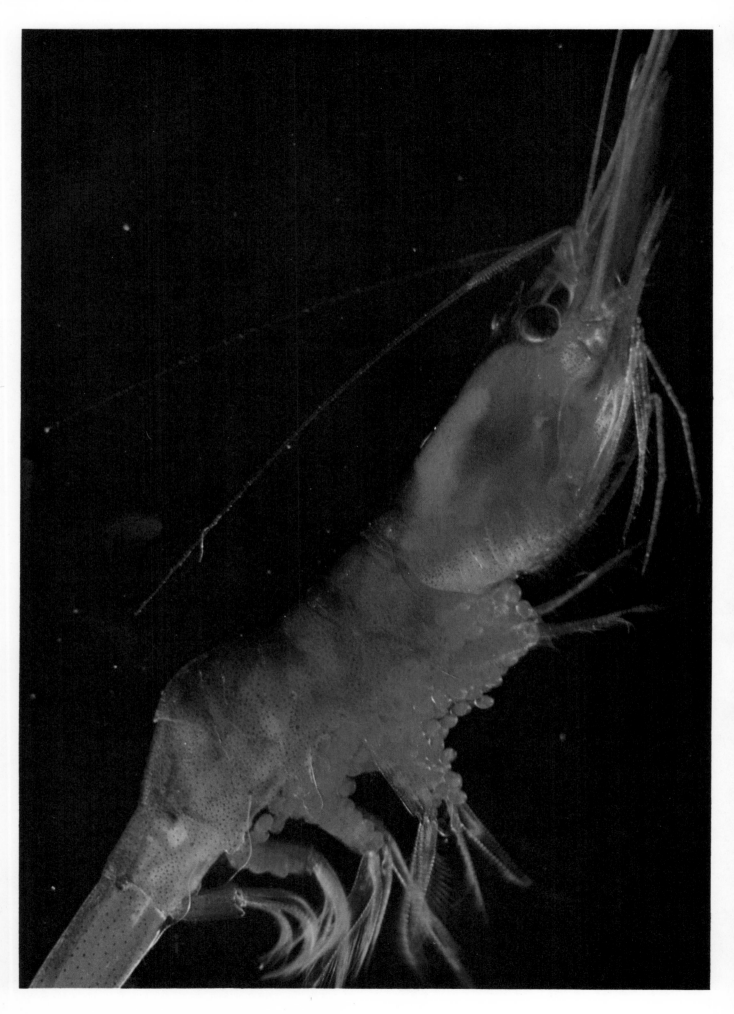

CRAB

There are something like 5,000 different kinds of crab and they are to be found in every ocean in the world. Some are small, less than half an inch across their tiny shells. By contrast, the giant crabs of Japan and Tasmania have legs that are as much as 3m (10 feet) long. They all belong to an order known as Decapoda which means that, despite their differences in size, all have 10 legs.

The **fiddler crab** has a name that comes from the fact he has one claw much larger than the other. He also uses his hind pair of legs as paddles.

PRAWN

The **prawn** is first cousin to the lobster and crab. There are several types of prawn, that shown being one that lives in very deep water. The female carries her eggs on the underside of her body and when they hatch they rise to the surface to live on tiny plankton. Then, when they are larger, they descend to the depths to join the other grown prawns and eat the same food. The chameleon prawn changes colour to match its surroundings; the snapping prawn makes a clapping sound with its large claw.

AMONGST THE CORAL

A wonder of the sea-bed is the beautiful coral which is usually found in tropical seas and warm, shallow waters. It consists of the skeletons of millions of tiny creatures called polyps. Coral reefs and atolls make wonderful hiding places for fish, two kinds of which are to be seen in this photograph. One is the **blue coral fish,** the other, more difficult to see, is the **transparent juvenile fish,** sheltering amongst stagshorn coral.

SEA-CREATURES WITH ARMS

For centuries there have been stories of giant sea-creatures with arms that drag down ships, so that a tasty meal of drowned seamen might follow. The animal concerned is not the octopus as one might expect, because it does not grow large enough. It is the giant squid, a near relation to the cuttlefish.

The squid has eight arms with suckers on them attached to its head, and two larger tentacles next to the arms which can extend a long way. It has a hard beak, hooked like a parrot's, and it uses this to tear at its prey once the tentacles have caught it. These ugly creatures can grow to a vast size. The largest one ever found

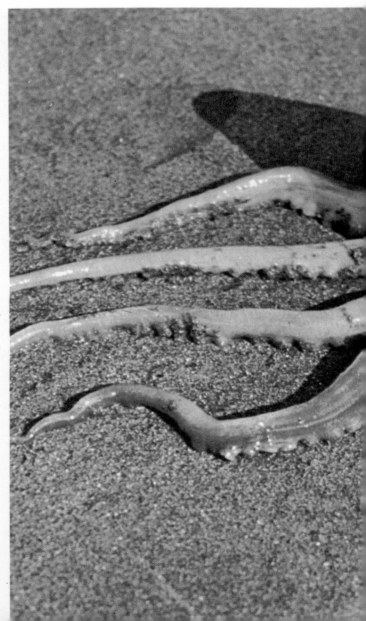

had a head and body 6m (20 feet) long and tentacles 11m (35 feet) long. It weighed roughly two tonnes.

The **cuttlefish** is very similar to the squid, and also related to the octopus. It is able to change colour according to what sort of rocks or underwater plants it is among. This helps it to avoid being caught by larger sea creatures such as whales, and helps it to catch its own food more easily. Its main food is shrimps, which it possibly attracts by means of small patches on its skin which glow in the dark. They are usually fairly small and can sometimes be seen in shoals at night. They live mainly in warm waters such as the Mediterranean.

The **octopus** rarely grows to more than a few feet in length although it can have an armspan of nearly 6m (20 feet). This gives it a very wide reach. Each arm or tentacle has about 300 carefully shaped suckers. Unlike the cuttlefish or squid it has only eight arms, not ten. On the whole it is rather a shy animal, preferring to hide among rocks and stony mud, waiting for a crab or some other little delicacy to come by. Octopuses prefer to live in the Mediterranean, in tropical waters near Australia, or in the coastal areas of the Pacific Ocean. Most types live entirely on shellfish.

EAGLE RAY

Some types of rays grow very large. The giant devil ray, for example, can reach a width of 6m (20 feet) and weigh over 1,600kg (3,500lb). One ray with attractive markings is known as the **eagle ray.**

A SHOCKING FISH

It is rather strange to think that the **electric ray** belongs to a type of large flat fish called 'torpedo'. Actually this name was taken from them to give to the weapon used by ships, submarines and aeroplanes. The electric ray is usually about 0.6m (2 feet) but can grow up to 1.8m (6 feet) in length. Some baby electric rays are shown. They live in several oceans and can release a very powerful electric shock, made all the more dangerous because it is sent through the water. It can be as strong as several hundred volts.

It leaps onto its prey, holds it with its fins, and releases the current to prevent the prey from moving.

Another fish that can be very dangerous belongs to the eel family – the **moray eel.** This grows to about 1.5m (5 feet) long but has a bite that can kill. In Roman times these eels were kept in special tanks and fed on dead slaves.

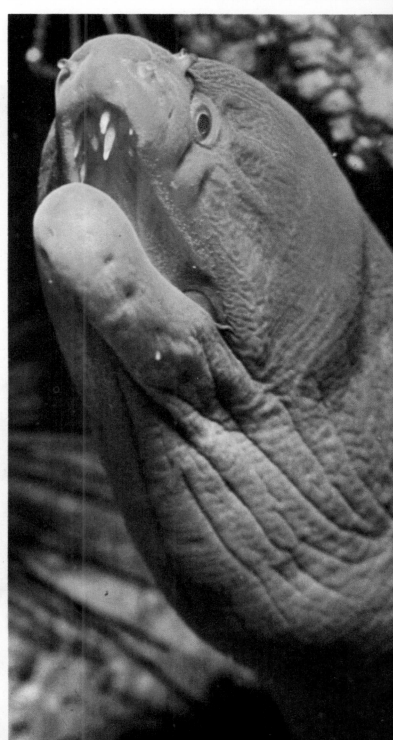

19

THE KILLERS

Sharks are thought to be the most dangerous of all fishes in the sea. So often in books and films they are very much the villains. With some sharks this is very true, but by no means for all. There are some 400 varieties of shark scattered throughout the world, yet only a few are dangerous. The main killers are the tiger shark, the blue shark and the hammerhead shark whilst the great white shark has another name, the 'man-eater'.

Yet even when sharks are harmless they are feared. Sailors believe that a shark following in the wake of a ship means that there will soon be the death of someone on board.

For the most part, the larger sharks live only in warm seas, where they lie near the surface. Indeed, one, the basking shark, spends most of its life drifting along at the surface, usually in the Mediterranean and the South Atlantic.

One very dangerous to man is the **great white shark** which can exceed 12m (40 feet) in length. Like the other killers, it has very powerful jaws whilst its mouth is large and set with rows of razor-sharp teeth which grow again as they wear out. Nowadays these terrible creatures are now very rare. Like most other sharks it has a lean, streamlined body and is a very powerful swimmer. And, like most sharks,

it will eat almost anything. When one was caught recently its stomach was found to contain – apart from all kinds of fish – some tin cans and some old shoes!

The **hammerhead shark** is a strange looking fish which can reach a length of 4.8m (16 feet). It is also a particularly dreaded hunter.

The larger hammerhead sharks, together with the great white and the mako sharks top the list in the US Navy's 'shark danger' ratings. And as long ago as 1593 another seaman, Richard Hawkins wrote: 'It is the most ravenous fishe knowne in the sea; for he swallowth all that hee findeth.' Yet Hawkins did not mention the many hundreds of types which are quite harmless.

By comparison, the **Pacific black tip shark** is very timid and does not dare to come close to a swimmer in the polynesian seas where it lives. It is a beautiful looking fish with a rounded snout and black patches at the end of its fins.

THE BIG ONES

Some members of the whale family are the largest of the giants that still exist today. They are strange creatures for they live in the sea, yet are mammals. Being mammals, they have to come up from time to time to breathe. When they reach the surface of the water they blow air from the top of their noses. This air is warm and moist and, when it meets the cold air, forms a kind of vapour. When this happens the whale is said to be 'blowing', although no water comes from the creature's nose or mouth.

There are two main types of whale—the whalebone and the toothed whales. The former are quite harmless for when they lose their baby teeth these are not replaced by more teeth but by the plates of whalebone known as 'baleen' hanging down from the roof of their mouths through which they sieve thousands of the tiny fishes upon which they live. A **grey whale** – a baleen, and a **white whale** (toothed) are shown. Such whales cruise along, at a very leisurely speed and often in schools as, for the most part, whales are very sociable creatures.

That cannot be said for the other group—the toothed whales. The fiercest of all of these is the rightly named **killer whale.** Although it rarely grows to more than 6m (20 feet), it wages war on every marine creature that may come its way. Killer whales are found all over the world but mostly in colder waters. They hunt in packs and sometimes six or so band together, surround a baleen whale, and tear it to pieces.

An even larger toothed whale is the sperm whale which may grow to be 18m (60 feet) long. This whale is hunted for its oil and for a substance called ambergris from which expensive perfumes are made. Sperm whales live mostly on squid and cuttlefish and usually need about a tonne of food a day. They also rise to the surface to 'blow' but the toothed whales have only one nostril whereas the baleens have two.

Dolphins are also members of the whale family.

The **common dolphin** usually moves in schools. They love to follow ships, leaping from the water almost as if they were showing off. Another type, the bottle-nosed dolphin, also likes to show off, but more generally in aquaria.

THE UGLY ONES

Unlike most other animals, there is but one species of **walrus.** They are found in both the Atlantic and Pacific Oceans, living at the edge of the Polar ice. Their name—walrus—is Scandinavian and means 'whale horse', but they are nothing like that elegant animal, the horse. The huge, clumsy body is covered with a tough, gnarled hide; it has short legs and flippers, which enable it to move on land. It falls easy prey to the Eskimos to whom it means life. Its hide covers their kayaks (canoes), the runners of their sledges are made from walrus bones and these, especially the tusks, go to make their spears, harpoons and fish-hooks. The fat is also used as fuel in their lamps.

The sea elephant is well named. A fully grown bull sea elephant can be well over 6m (20 feet) long and weigh four tonnes—little less than its namesake on land. It now lives in Antarctic waters. At one time it was found in many other of the world's oceans but it has been hunted almost to extinction, because its hide and oil are so valuable. Curiously, its name comes not from its vast size but from a short trunk which can be as long as 750mm (30 in). It lives entirely on fish and though several zoos have taken sea elephants into their aquaria, they are rare nowadays being expensive to keep as they eat such enormous amounts of fish! The **southern sea elephant,** yawning perhaps, is shown here.

NORTHERN SEA ELEPHANT

The **northern sea elephant** is smaller than its 'cousin', the southern sea elephant, both in size and in numbers. There was a time when there were thousands of these creatures on Guadalupe Island but its hide and oil made it the target for generations of fishermen.

MANATEE (SEA COW)

This strange creature is a large mammal growing up to 4.5m (15 feet) in length. It prefers the estuaries of large rivers, living on seaweed and other water plants. Usually quiet animals, they can become dangerous for when attacked by fishermen will often upset the boat.

GALAPAGOS SEALIONS

These young **Galapagos sealions** romp amongst the warm surf as it washes against the rocks that fringe Las Plazas, off the western coast of South America. They seem to be sharing their fun with some red Sallylightfoot crabs. Many seals do this especially the Californian (Galapagos) sealions which perform in circuses.

The land dwellers

All animal life falls into two great groups—the warm-blooded and the cold-blooded. Mammals and birds are in the first, and fish, amphibia and reptiles are in the second.

Let us now look at some of the land dwellers in detail.

CAMEL

This animal has served man faithfully in the desert regions for centuries. There are two types: the one-humped camel of a family to which the **dromedary** belongs, and the bactrian camel known by its double hump. Arabs feed on its rich milk, make their clothing from its thick hair and use its skin for tents and saddles.

PIG

The pig belongs to a group of even-toed ungulates (*ungulata* meaning 'hoofed'), one of man's most important species for it includes the domestic animals which have given him food, drink and clothing for centuries. The pigs shown here are rather charming **Vietnamese pot-bellied pigs.**

GOAT

Goats are members of the same group and, like the pigs, have been in man's service for at least 6,000 years, being prized for their flesh, milk and coats. There are still wild goats, the ibex being the best known. There is also the angora goat with its beautiful silky hair known as 'mohair'.

CHIMPANZEE

The **chimpanzee's** home is in tropical Africa. It is a member of the family of the great apes which also includes the gorilla, orang-utan and the pygmy chimpanzee. Although its home is in the forest, it lives partly on the ground, travelling with its tribe. It moves mainly at dusk and dawn, the forest becoming filled with the most hideous noise as the band keep together. Chimpanzees have always been a favourite with everyone, ever since the first was brought to London in the year of 1740. Of all the animals, the chimpanzee is the most human in looks and intelligence.

BEAUTIFUL CREATURES

A number of the Antelope family are shown together. The **gerenuk,** or giraffe antelope, is a very delicate looking animal and can live far from water in East Africa using the moisture from the leaves it feeds on. Although gerenuks are scarcely over 1m (3 feet) tall, when they pick leaves

they raise themselves on their hind legs, adding as much again to their height.

The **eland** is a much heavier animal, weighing up to 900kg (2,000lb). Small herds of these may be seen on the edge of the grasslands in East and South Africa. They are very agile creatures and can jump more than 1.8m (6 feet) high—about their own height. Another native of Africa is the **hartebeest,** one of the larger antelopes. It is one of the first animals to die without water. Hartebeests travel in herds, up to 20 animals being led by an old bull.

The most graceful of all antelopes is the **impala.** It is very fond of company and its herd can sometimes number 500 or so of these beautiful little animals.

WART HOG

If the antelope is one of nature's most lovely animals, the **wart hog** is one of the ugliest. A type of African pig, feeding on grass, sedge and tubers. The body is mainly hairless, except for the neck and back which have long, bristly hair. But it is the head which is so ugly. It is very large with bulbous eyes high on the head. It can almost look behind without turning its head. The boar also has four tusks and at each side of the face are large pads that look so much like warts that they have given the animal its name.

PRAIRIE DOG

This funny little fellow does not look like a dog at all. It is thought that its name came from the bark-like sound it makes when alarmed. It is also called the barking squirrel. It inhabits the prairies to the east of the Rocky Mountains and there was a time when billions of **prairie dogs** covered all the North American plains with their huge 'dog towns.' Now there are few left, thanks to hunting, poisoning and so on. Yet they are still very sociable animals, building their burrows and being very friendly with their neighbours.

BROWN BEAR

There are many members of the bear family and they are spread all over the world. Some of them are more than just large . . . they are giants! The largest of all is Alaska's **brown bear,** which is often nearly 3m (10 feet) long with a weight of more than half a tonne. But, like all bears, it is not savage unless attacked or if it thinks its cubs are in danger. Like many other bears it does not hunt but ambles along, scratching up a root here, picking and munching some wild fruit there, eating the wild honey which it loves, occasionally catching a fish from the river with its paw.

Some experts doubt whether bears ever kill for food anything much larger than a baby antelope but when they fight they are very dangerous, for the brown bear can knock down an ox with a single blow from one of its fore-paws.

KANGAROO

When the earth was still changing shape, the continent of Australia became separated from other land masses. In consequence, many of Australia's animals—the duck-billed platypus, the koala bear, the wombat and the kangaroo are found nowhere else. Of them all, the **kangaroo** is the animal that people think of when they think of Australia. It is shown on that country's coat-of-arms.

Somebody once said the kangaroo was a mother with a built-in pram! Kangaroos are called marsupials (from the Latin *marsupium* meaning pouch). Every female kangaroo has this pouch beneath her stomach and protects her new-born baby within it until it is at least four months old. Even when it is older it will jump back when danger threatens. The kangaroo's tail is also very important. It sits on it when resting and uses the tail for balance when making its great leaps.

LION

The **lion** is truly the King of Beasts. Large, often weighing more than 225kg (500lb), it can pull down any animal except the elephant and the rhinoceros. In its wild state it is now only seen in the central region of Africa although, for many years, it was also a native of India. But the British in the early part of this century unfortunately cleared that country of this fine beast—one officer alone bagging no fewer than 80 lions in three years!

Although it usually only attacks other animals it can also become a 'man-eater' when it grows old and cannot chase antelopes or master the powerful buffalo. Yet it is a very sociable animal—amongst its own kind—and often hunts in packs or 'prides'; often made up of two lions, and a few lionesses with their cubs.

TIGER

The **tiger** is to India what the lion is to Africa. Both animals are roughly the same size although the tiger's coat is more beautiful. It has stripes, dark on a rich yellow ground. The tiger may look pretty but is a very blood-thirsty animal. It has massive jaws with great fangs and eyes that make its victim tremble. As one experienced hunter said: 'That green glare of a tiger's eyes at close quarters has a distinctly unsettling effect on the nerves.'

In one thing the tiger exceeds the lion. Man-eating lions are rare—but man-eating tigers are common and have been known to kill several villagers.

WILD CAT

At first glance, the **wild cat** looks very like

the friendly tabby which curls up before so many firesides. But it is really very different for it is a vicious creature, and often attacks man, though usually in self-defence. Its food generally, however, consists of birds and rodents. It is usually found in wooded areas, far from the haunts of man in such places as France, Italy and Russia. Like the tiger, it prefers to hunt at night, creeping silently and stealthily upon its victim. Although the wild cat of Europe is one of Britain's oldest dwellers, it was never seen in Ireland. It is now extinct in England but can still be seen in parts of Scotland, though sometimes these turn out to be tame cats that have left their homes for a free life in the woods. In this state they can be very dangerous and fierce.

Usually its thick fur is of a yellow colour with a black streak.

TERRIERS

Two little dogs shown on the famous Bayeux tapestry are meant to be terriers. This shows that they have been used, mainly to chase vermin in Britain, since Norman times. They are still hard-working dogs. There are now several breeds, some rough haired, and others smooth. At one time the bull-terrier was thought of as a dog that kept company with rogues and criminals. The terrier shown here has the name **Bedlington,** given to the breed in 1825 by a mason named Joseph Aynsley Bedlington.

DALMATIAN

Before motor-cars were seen on the roads, the attractively spotted **dalmatian** was known as the coach dog. This was because it was trained to follow carriages, usually living in the stables with the horses and going out with them on exercise. Very often it would run between the wheels of its master's carriage for miles, easily keeping up with the horses. Until 1800, dalmatians were used as sporting dogs but since then have been kept purely as pets and companions. They first came to Britain in the middle of the 18th century from Dalmatia.

HUSKY

This dog is one of the world's hardest working and most useful. It is found mainly in Arctic regions where it is generally used as a sled dog. There is much of the wolf about him because many **huskies** have been crossed with timber wolves. Some of the strongest and fiercest of these dogs belong to the Eskimos, yet the puppy in the picture looks deceptively gentle and sweet. A team of huskies can pull heavy loads for several hours at a time.

POINTER

The **pointer** is now found all over the world, yet it first came from Spain in 1600. It was first brought into Britain about 250 years ago when men began using guns to shoot down game-birds. The modern pointer has come from crossing the dog with the foxhound and greyhound. Pointers usually work in pairs and when one first scents the bird he 'freezes', pointing with his nose to where it is to be found whilst the other lies down and waits.

KOMMONDORE

There are a number of large sheepdogs used in various parts of the Continent which are rarely seen elsewhere. They are like huge mastiffs and, for the most part, are used to protect their master's sheep against wolves and other fierce animals. The breeds found in Russia and Hungary are the largest known dogs and are very strong and vicious. Two Hungarian dogs, the kuvasz and the kommondore are very similar, the former being the largest dog in the world. The **kommondore** has a strange coat for it seems to be a mass of thick cords rather than the usual hair.

PENGUIN

It may seem very strange to call the penguin a bird for although it has wings, it cannot fly. The strange creature, looking at a distance like a waiter in evening dress, is found entirely in the Southern Hemisphere. Their wings are more like paddles, covered with scaly feathers. The largest of the species is the **emperor penguin** which may stand well over 1.2m (4 feet) high and lives on the Antarctic pack ice, near the South Pole. Penguins spend much of their life in the sea, moving with a rare turn of speed, using their wings like flippers under the water.

King penguins live a little farther south, on the islands of the Antarctic. Most penguins lay their eggs in burrows or make simple nest mounds of grass, beach debris or just stones. The hen of the king penguin lays only one egg at a time which it hatches by keeping it warm between its legs. If it becomes alarmed, it will shuffle away, carrying the egg with it. When the hen has to go off to wash or feed, the male bird takes over. They do this by placing their toes together and rolling the egg from one to the other, using their beaks to set it in place.

OSTRICH

Another non-flying bird is the **ostrich.** It is found in Africa and South West Asia and the males, being 2.4m (8 feet) high and weighing about 135kg (300 lb) make it the largest living bird. They have black body-feathers and white wing-feathers whilst the hens are a dusky grey. Their plumes have been worn as decoration since ancient times. It is a very powerful fighter, being the only bird known to have attacked and killed men in self-defence. Its weapon is its heavy foot. This has only two toes and the big one has a shape very like a hoof. With its long legs and powerful thigh muscles, the ostrich can kill many of its enemies with a single kick. It is also one of the fastest runners of all birds. The large egg of the ostrich makes a tasty omelette for more than a dozen people. The cock bird stands guard over the eggs – laid by 3 or 4 hens in the same nest – until they are hatched, ready to use his foot on any creature that tries to steal them.

There is a saying about 'burying your head in the sand like an ostrich'. Actually the ostrich sinks to the ground when pursued and then is difficult to see. So it is not so foolish after all.

TREE FROG

The staring eyes of this strange frog are on the look-out for any insect that might come its way. Then, when the insect is within reach the frog leaps at it, catching it in its mouth. This is quite a brave thing to do for this particular frog lives in trees sometimes a very long way from the ground. As it sails through the air it relies on its hands and feet, all fitted with special discs to make them stick onto the nearest leaf or branch, thus breaking its fall.

DESERT SIDE-WINDING ADDER

Most snakes move along the ground, head first, making a series of wriggles. This strange adder, does not move this way at all but sideways, the better to move through loose stones and sand.

NILE CROCODILE

Here, taking its first look at a new and strange world, is a baby crocodile. He and the family in the other eggs will be lucky to stay alive for at this moment they are easy prey for birds. The eggs are laid ashore in buried nests, and incubated for 2-3 months, carefully guarded by the female. About 60 eggs are put in a nest. The crocodile is a cold-blooded reptile, which lives happily in water and on dry land. The young come out of the eggs as complete little crocodiles about 20-25cm (8-10 in) long. Adult crocodiles can grow up to 6m (20 feet) in length and may live for up to 100 years.

Generally crocodiles are of little danger to man except the **Nile crocodile** which has killed many people.

COMMON LIZARD
This dragon-like creature appears in many parts of Europe and Asia and is the only reptile found in Ireland. The males of this species are about 15cm (6 inches) long, their tail taking up half their length. They dig holes in the autumn and hibernate in them until the spring.

GREEN IGUANA
Another member of the lizard family is the **green iguana.** It lives mainly in northern and central South America and grows to a length of 1.8m (6 feet), which includes its very long tail. These creatures will often climb trees after insects.

COMMON TOAD
Toads rarely return to water except during the breeding season for their dull and wrinkled skins do not need so much moisture as frogs. They seek food mostly after dark, and spend most of the day in holes where it is cool and damp.

Birds of the air

Birds have been on this earth for more than 150 million years. It is no wonder that we now see so many different varieties all over the world—some that fly, some that, like the ostrich are earth-bound, and some that are more at home in the sea from which, originally, they came as reptiles which finally grew wings. Let us now look at some of the inhabitants of this amazing world of birds.

PRAIRIE CHICKEN

Like so many other breeds of birds, that known as the **prairie chicken** is in danger of dying out altogether. Prairie fires that destroy acres of the tall American grass are the main cause. This bird is very amusing to watch for he does a stamping dance during which he raises and spreads his tail whilst making a strange, booming sound.

FLAMINGO

This beautiful bird offers one of the most amazing sights in the whole of nature. During the breeding season these colourful birds gather together in East Africa's Rift Valley. There they feed on the lakes in huge colonies – sometimes more than a million birds can be seen together, their lovely plumage ranging from pure white to the deepest red.

ROBIN

This is a very popular bird and one which is shown on many cards at Christmas time. The **robin** sings all the year round, except for a spell in July when he is moulting. His song is to protect his territory. He is common in Britain and other parts of Northern Europe. The robin is often very tame, and will search for worms and other small animals within inches of a gardener.

The red breast is important as a warning signal to other birds if they try to encroach on his territory.

DUNNOCK

Often called the 'hedge sparrow' the **dunnock** is not a sparrow, though it looks similar. Found in Europe, Asia and Africa, it lives in the undergrowth in woods, hedgerows and scrubland, and is tame enough to be found in parks and gardens. The male and female look alike, and their 'dun' colouring (grey breast and brown striped back) give the bird its name. Dunnocks feed mainly on insect life, grubs and spiders, but eat seeds when no other food is available. The nests are made of grass and moss, containing 4-6 bright blue eggs.

WREN

The little **wren** lives its life in the country, usually near people's homes. Its bright and lively movements have made it a great favourite with people as they watch it cheerfully hop along with its cocked up tail.

At the beginning of the breeding season, the male wren builds several nests, and the female then selects one in which to lay her eggs. The nest is neat and flexible, with a domed top, and is sometimes built among the roots of fallen trees. The wren is one of the loudest birds in the dawn chorus, although it is so small.

SWAN

The **swan** is called a Royal bird—and it has marks to prove it. For centuries all swans in Britain belonged to the king and queen of the time, a privilege now shared with the Vintners and Dyers Guilds. The marking, still done even today on the Thames between London and Windsor, is known as 'swan upping'. It was long thought a serious crime to tamper with the bird, an offender being sent to prison for a year and a day, and also fined. There is a tradition that, when dying, a swan sings a sad, sweet song, whereas during the rest of his life he is always silent.

There are eight different types of swans. They are to be seen in most parts of the world. They are generally white in colour, one exception being the black swans of Australia which are the official emblem of Western Australia. Europe's common or 'mute' swan is said never to use its voice in captivity. It makes its nests on the lakes and swamps of much of northern and central Europe and Asia. Another that yearly visits Britain and other parts of Europe from the Arctic is the whooper, or whistling swan.

KITTIWAKE

This is a gull that is unlike other gulls—it takes *all* its food from the sea. Other gulls may be seen in their hundreds around markets, rubbish dumps and so on. The **kittiwake,** however, is always far out at sea, following trawlers, and rarely comes to land except to breed. Its nest is also quite different from those of other gulls. It is cup-shaped and attached by mud onto steep cliff faces. The bird's claws are sharper and longer than those of other gulls which means it can hang onto the sides of cliffs whilst feeding its young. The young kittiwakes, safe in their nest, stay there for at least six weeks before they try to fly. Young kittiwakes have unusual black 'Vs' which stretch the length of either wing. The name of these birds comes from their unusual cry, which sounds rather like 'kittiwake'.

ARCTIC TERN
Terns look very like gulls but they are smaller and usually with long, forked tails. The **Arctic tern** is unusual, for it breeds in the far north and migrates south in the autumn. It sets out from the Arctic, breeds in Britain and other nearby countries, then winters 10,000 miles away in the Antarctic.

PUFFINS
The **puffin** is a funny-looking bird, short and stubby, with a black and white body and a bill that is red, blue and yellow which makes it look like a clown. Yet this bill is important, for it uses it to attract a mate. The puffin usually spends its winter at sea, and is almost as good at swimming underwater, using its wings as flippers, as it is at flying in the air.

▲ AFRICAN SPOONBILL

There are a great number of these wading birds that live in lagoons and marshes, many of them in Africa, although at one time they used to breed in Britain. The Bishop of Fulham forbade anyone to take spoonbills from nests on his estate, but that was in 1523! They no longer breed in Britain but often come as summer visitors. They take their name, of course, from their strangely shaped bills. Shaped like spoons, the birds sweep them from side to side, scooping up small fishes and insects. Like the flamingo, they gather in huge colonies in Africa.

STORK

The stork, an extremely long-legged bird, is one whose presence is thought to be a sign of good luck wherever it is found. They are familiar in northern Europe where they nest on roofs or balanced on chimney-tops. They make large, round nests, built of twigs, earth and grass, and each year a new nest is built on the remains of the old one. Its history is a long one. The Egyptians paid it the same respect as they did their sacred ibis; a Greek law which made children keep their parents in old age was named after the bird; the Romans thought it a bird bringing good luck. Of them all, the **marabou stork**  is the least attractive. It lives in East Africa and feeds on carrion and rubbish, acting as a kind of unpaid dustbin man! Yet it can be a very dangerous bird for its long and sharp bill is greatly feared by other birds, even the hungry vulture dares not attack it.

SNAKE BIRD

This strange bird is called the **snake bird,** not because it kills snakes but because of the snake-like movement of its long neck when it swims or hunts. It dives into the water until it spots its prey and then thrusts out its long, snake-like neck, spearing the fish on the end of its bill. As soon as the snake bird has the struggling fish safely on the end of its pointed bill, it comes to the surface and heads for dry land. It kills the fish by banging it upon a stone, then swallows it, head first.

It cannot stay in the water very long otherwise its feathers become water-logged. When this happens it climbs onto the bank and spreads its wet wings so that they quickly dry in the sun.

TOUCAN

In the great forests of the Amazon live some of the strangest and most colourful birds on earth. One of the strangest is the **toucan.** It has a bill which is as long as its body and usually a bright yellow.

◀ CANADA GOOSE

This beautiful bird came to Britain in a strange way. Early settlers in North America were charmed by this, the largest goose, with its striking black head and which bred in places from Labrador to Alaska. Some were shipped back to Britain about 250 years ago. Later, some escaped

from the estates of collectors to become wild birds. Since then they have bred in large numbers, and have now become quite common.

HUMMING BIRDS

These lovely little birds, of which there are many types, are found in North and South America. Some measure only 6cm (2.5in) from beak to tail. They are so swift in flight that they are often almost impossible to see. They feed on the nectar of flowers, carrying the pollen from one flower to another, like bees.

VILLAGE WEAVER

These strange birds have been given their name because of the wonderful way they prepare their nests – all very finely woven. Their nests vary slightly according to the type of weaver. Some weavers, for example, build a common nest in which each pair has a separate cavity with its own entrance, like a block of flats! Others make separate bottle-shaped nests, some adding clay to make them heavier and stop them swaying in the wind.

BEE-EATER

The brightly coloured **bee-eater** lives in Asia, Australia and Europe. Another type of bee-eater from Africa migrates to Europe every year, from late spring to early autumn. They are just under 30cm (12in) long with long pointed wings and with brilliantly coloured heads and bodies. At

times they are mistaken for kingfishers. They have strong and pointed beaks with which they dig holes in river banks and then build their nests far inside. From these hide-outs they set off to catch and eat their favourite meal – bees. As they look for their meal they dart and swoop in a charming way, a way that has earned them the name of 'golden swallows'. There are several types of bee-eater. One is chestnut, gold and green above, gold and black below with green, black and chestnut wings and a green tail. Another, the blue-tailed bee-eater, has a delightful blue tail and chestnut throat.

LOVE-BIRDS
This delightful name is given to a group of small and pretty parrots who always perch very close together. One group of **love-birds** come from Africa and the rosy-faced ▼

love-bird, about 15cm (6in) long, is a very popular cage bird.

COCKATOO
This pretty member of the parrot family can always be recognized by the crest of feathers sticking upright on its head. There are several types of this colourful bird including the greater sulphur-crested, first seen on Captain Cook's voyage to Australia in the 1770s; the great white cockatoo, a native of the Moluccas; and Leadbeater's cockatoo. This latter is a white and pink bird which opens its crest when it becomes excited. This crest is seen to be in the Spanish national colours – hence its other name, the Spanish Flag. Cockatoos are to be seen in most zoos around the world and their antics are very amusing to watch. This is the **sulphur-crested cockatoo.** ▼

SECRETARY BIRD

This strange long-legged bird stands nearly 1.2m (4 feet) high. It is found only in Africa, mainly south of the Sahara. Its name comes from the tufts at the back of the head which look like quill pens stuck behind the ear. It is of great use to man, being a killer of venomous snakes. When it sights one it swoops down and strikes at it with the talons of its long legs until the snake is dead.

BARN OWLS

The adult **barn owl** is golden buff with a white face, chest and legs. Here are young owls that still have the creamy down of the newly hatched. The barn owl does not rely on sight – its wonderful hearing helps it to pick out its prey on the darkest night. Instead of nests the eggs are laid on a heap made from the fur, feathers and bones of the owl's victims.

MONKEY EAGLE

This fine-looking bird has short wings, unlike those of other eagles. This helps it to fly quickly through branches of trees where the monkeys hide. Its beak, more hooked than other eagles, is so sharp that it can kill its prey with one terrible bite. It lives in the deep forests of the Philippines but is steadily becoming rarer.

GOLDEN EAGLE

This is truly the king of birds. Nation after nation, from ancient Assyria to modern Germany have used it as a royal crest or military standard. In captivity the bird has a wild majesty but it is best when, high overhead, its scans sky and ground for its quarry. It then launches itself at its prey at a speed of 145km/h (90 mph) – and rarely misses! It nests in places almost impossible to reach, usually high up on some mountain crag or on a sea cliff ledge.

Giants
and midgets

Just as amongst humans, the animal kingdom has its giants and its midgets. Of all living land animals, the largest by far is the African elephant; the tallest is the giraffe which sometimes measures over 5.5m (18 feet) from top to toe. The smallest land mammal is the pygmy shrew weighing just over 15gm (0.5oz). In the sea swims the largest of all mammals, the blue whale whilst the largest *fish* is the whale shark. Now let us take a look at the animal kingdom and study the big and the little.

ELEPHANT

There are two main types of elephant living today, the Indian and the **African elephant.** The former, originally, was used in war, going into battle carrying armed warriors. Alexander the Great invaded India in the 3rd century B.C. to meet 'elephants bearing castles of trees on their backs.' Being told that the elephant was afraid of pigs he placed a herd of swine before his army which caused the elephants to turn and fly. Even today Indian elephants still do much heavy work, especially in the forests of Burma where they haul timber.

The largest elephant and, indeed, the largest land animal is the African, standing well over 3m (10 feet) and with large ears, whereas those of the Indian are much smaller.

GIRAFFE

When early travellers returned to Europe with stories about the **giraffe,** no one would believe them. And no wonder. Who

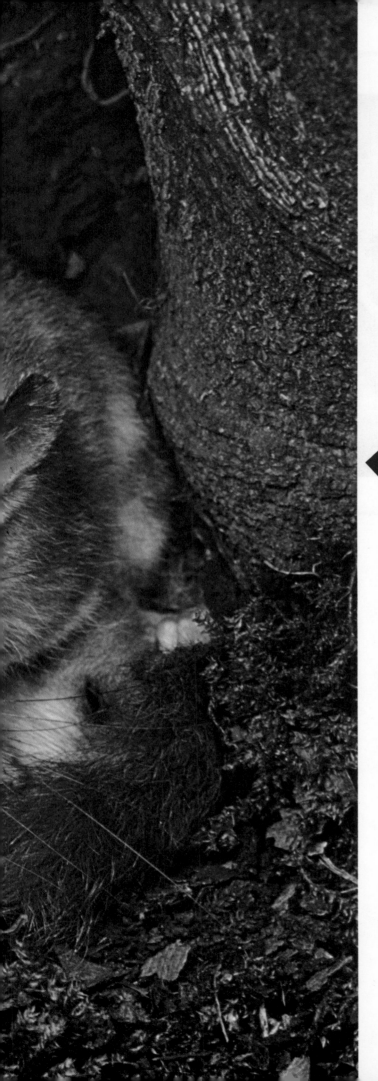

would believe tales of an animal that is like no other? It is the tallest animal with its head splendidly set on a long, tapering neck and with soft and gentle eyes. There are several types, all found in Africa. Both males and females have two or four horn-like knobs on the top of their heads, and sometimes other knobs on the forehead.

DORMOUSE

The dormouse, shown here with its young is an elegant little creature. It rarely grows larger than 6cm (2.5in) in length, with a tail as long again. Its diet is mainly of fruit, acorns, leaves and insects, much of which it stores up ready for its winter sleep (hibernation). When the cold weather comes it rolls itself up into its nest and falls into a kind of heavy doze from which it wakes from time to time for a snack. The one shown is the **common dormouse** but there are many different species. There are African, Japanese, Malabar and the Chinese pygmy dormouse and even one that lives in South-West Asia called the mouse-like dormouse!

THE FLEA

This tiny little insect has been the cause of more deaths than any creature which has ever lived. This is because fleas, which live on other animals, carry disease and plague from one creature to another. In Europe, in the Middle Ages, fleas caused the deaths of more than 25 million people!

LEMUR

A close relative of monkeys, lemurs are found only on Madagascar and a few islands nearby. One type is the smallest of all primates, some weighing as little as 45gm (1.6oz) and measuring about 6cm (2½in) long, including the tail. The best known is the ring-tailed lemur which is about the size of a cat and, curiously, has a miaouw just like one! It is just as much at home on the ground as in the trees where it usually lives.

Another small member of the family is the brown mouse lemur, most being little bigger than house mice. Some dwarf lemurs living in areas which have droughts will survive by going into a kind of deep sleep. The **lesser mouse lemur** is the smallest of them all, and during the difficult dry season, it also is a great sleeper, feeding itself from fatty food which it stores away inside its large and swollen tail.

ORANG-UTAN

The name of this strange creature comes from two Malay words which mean 'Man of the Woods'. For the most part it lives in the forests of Borneo and Sumatra. It grows to about 1.2m (4 feet) high, with long arms and short legs and a face, as you can see, which is far from handsome. It finds it difficult to walk, for its arms are twice that of its height, reaching up to 2.5m (8 feet). If it has to cross a place where there are no trees, it rests its knuckles on the ground and swings its body through the arms as if it was on crutches. But in the trees it is one of the nimblest of animals, leaping from tree to tree at great speed, the mothers carrying their young as they go. Unlike other members of the great ape family it does not travel in bands but prefers to live alone, eating mainly fruit, leaves and young shoots.

THE BIG APE

The gorilla is the largest and strongest of all members of the ape family. It is just under 1.8m (6 feet) high and has been known to weigh more than 250kg (40 stone). It walks upright on its hind legs far more than any other ape. Because of this, early explorers believed the gorilla, seen in the dim light of the forest, was some kind of huge, hair-covered savage.

When Hanno, an explorer from Carthage visited Africa in 350 B.C., some furry creatures hurled stones at him from the side of a mountain. He gave them the name of 'gorilla'. There is no doubt now, however, that they were really baboons. Some 2,000 years later, in 1848, the skull of a huge animal was brought to Britain from Africa and its finder stated it was that of a gorilla, but it was not until a live one was brought to Europe in 1876 that he was found to be right. None were found earlier because the gorilla, for all his terrifying looks and the way he beats his huge chest when cornered, is really a very shy animal.

They are so rare that it was not until 1959 that the first thorough study of these strange animals took place. This was by a team led by George Schaller of the New York Zoological Society. Although the work was difficult—for the gorillas would flee at the first sight of the humans—much was discovered. It was proved that gorillas, for all their terrifying size and looks, live happily together, do not fight amongst themselves and that no other animal preys upon them. They also do not prey on other animals for they are vegetarians and live on palm shoots, bananas, fruit and nuts. Each troop is led by an old gorilla who remains its head until another finally takes his place.

Yet as the population of Africa grows so the great forests that have given these animals shelter for thousands of years are slowly being cut down. It may well be that, in years to come, the only gorillas to be seen, either the lowland or the **mountain gorilla,** may well be in zoos throughout the world. Great work in zoos has been done. In 1956, in Columbus, Ohio, a baby gorilla was born—the first ever in captivity. London Zoo also has a fine male gorilla, 'Guy', who lives happily with his mate. The world's largest collection, however, is in the Ibadan Zoo in Nigeria, where visitors stand for hours happily watching the animals romping with each other or sometimes 'helping' the workmen as they use pick and shovel.

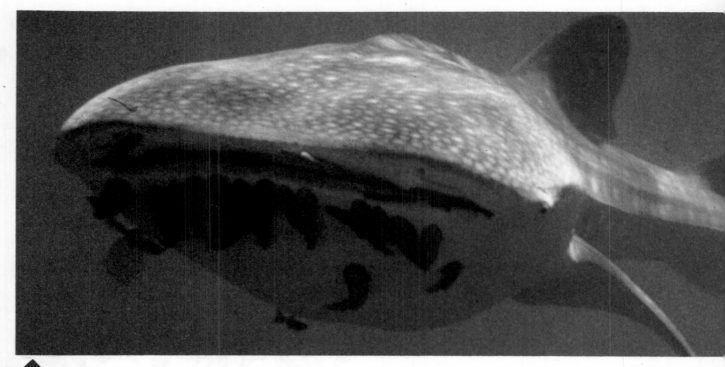

WHALE SHARK

This is the biggest fish in the sea. It has a long body and a broad head and, along its upper part, strange ridges. One line of these runs along the middle of its back, with two or three on either side. Its large straight mouth is armed with a great number of small teeth. It is usually brown or grey, whilst both head and body are covered with round white spots. It was first discovered near the Cape of Good Hope, Africa, more than 150 years ago and at first the fisherman who harpooned it could hardly believe he had caught such a vast creature. Later, one that measured nearly 18m (60 feet) with a weight of over 41 tonnes was caught in a fish-trap in the Gulf of Siam.

In spite of the fact that it is by far the largest fish, however, it is quite harmless, and only an accidental bump from its huge body can cause damage to a boat. It can easily be approached and harpooned but, when wounded, usually dives straight down, dragging the boat behind it. It feeds on small crustaceans (crabs, lobsters and shrimps) and large quantities of plankton.

BLUE WHALE

As we have already seen, the members of the whale family are not fishes but mammals. The largest of the family is the largest mammal in existence. This is the great **blue whale,** the largest creature on earth—or should it be in the sea—which makes all other mammals seem small by comparison. It lives in the waters of the Antarctic and is often more than 30m (100 feet) long, whilst some have been known to weigh as much as 150 tonnes, and that can be more than 30 times the weight of an elephant! As far as we can tell, the blue whale is not only the largest living animal on the earth today but the largest that has ever lived. And that includes the dinosaurs of ancient times.

The blue whale is finely shaped and

its whole appearance gives the feeling that it can swim really fast when it needs to. Its head is less than a quarter of its body length and while it is still huge, gives a slimmer, more 'stream-lined' look to the creature than most sperm whales. It is only when the creature has been killed and hauled ashore that an idea of its vast size can be gained.

▶PLANKTON

We have heard much about **plankton** the food of many sea-creatures, including the blue whale and the whale shark. So what is it? Plankton are minute, shrimp-like creatures which drift on the surface of the sea. The baleen whales and the whale sharks suck in the water that is filled with these tiny creatures, drain it again through the matted inner part of the baleen blades back into the sea, leaving the plankton within their mouths. Each whale eats several tons of plankton a day, yet there are always plenty of these tiny creatures to take their place. When conditions are right they can double their numbers daily until the sea becomes covered with them. Herring and mackerel also feed on plankton, and other creatures such as crabs and shell-fish, which live on the sea bed, are fed by dead or dying plankton which rain down from the surface. Obviously, plankton are very vital creatures to have in the sea.

OUR FRIEND, THE HORSE

Of all animals known to man, the horse has proved the most useful and the most faithful. The first to tame this fine animal were the Aryans, men who lived on the great grass-lands lying between Europe and Asia. Old records show that for many centuries the horse was not ridden but used to draw chariots. It slowly spread across the Middle East to Europe, playing a most important part in warfare, but also doing useful work on the farms and in carrying people from place to place.

Horses range very greatly in size. The smallest is the little **Shetland pony.** It is rarely more than eight hands high (10cm (4in) is equal to one 'hand') but it is very hardy and very friendly. It has a warm shaggy coat which protects it against severe winter weather. Being the smallest horse in the whole equine kingdom, no wonder it is such a great favourite with children.

By contrast, this large, powerful horse is the fine **shire horse.** It proved very useful during the Middle Ages for it was the only horse able to lumber into battle carrying a knight in full armour, on top of its own armour. It all added up to about a quarter of a tonne! When armour fell out of fashion the shire horse proved—and are still proving—to be ideal for farm work. The size, strength, courage and docility of this breed of horse have been developed till we now have an animal ideal for heavy work. They are often used now by brewery companies, partly for advertising purposes.

One shire horse used by an English brewery stood over eighteen hands high and weighed more than a tonne.

THE BIG AND THE LITTLE

There are hundreds of different types of dogs and the way they range from the very large to the very small is like that of the horse—perhaps even more so. It is interesting to think for a moment what work many of the dogs we have as pets today were once bred to do. The great dane, for example, was trained to hunt boars; the dachshund was a hunter of badgers; the beautiful borzoi was, in its native Russia, a brave hunter of the wolf and the bear; whilst in ancient times the mastiff was used to hunt lions! Such dogs were allowed to grow to great sizes so that they could face any wild animal that might attack them.

The huge and beautiful white-coated **Pyrenean dog** is basically a mastiff and is still used as a guard against wolves throughout the mountain ranges of northern Europe. They are shepherd dogs—guard dogs—rather than sheep dogs, which are used for actually rounding up sheep.

A similar looking dog, but one first used to bring help to lost and freezing travellers is the delightful and friendly **St. Bernard.** It is descended from the Alpine mastiffs which were kept at the Hospice of

Great St. Bernard in Switzerland. These dogs have saved hundreds of lives. One, named Barry, rescued more than 40 people who had lost their way whilst trying to cross the Alps in bad weather. The St. Bernard is a mountain dog, large, strong and well able to push its way through deep, clinging snow. It is also the heaviest breed of all domestic dogs—one weighed 135kg (21 stone)!

In contrast is the attractive little **Jack Russell,** named after the Rev. John Russell of Devon who bred this very small dog, which has become one of the most popular of all such small breeds.

'TOY' DOGS

There are a number of charming little dogs which have the name 'toy' dogs. This name is given to such as the chihuahua of Mexico, the world's smallest dog which often weighs little over 0.5kg (1lb); the English toy terrier, never more than 3.5kg (8lb) when fully grown; the tiny Yorkshire terrier, the Japanese spaniel and the charming King Charles spaniel.

Probably the most popular toy dog is the **Pekinese.** This delightful dog has a strange history. 3,000 years ago it lived in China and from figures, carvings and paintings it can be seen that it has not changed at all. It is still the same blunt-muzzled bundle of fur.

IRISH WOLFHOUND

Another dog whose ancestry goes back many years is the large **Irish wolfhound,** for years regarded as the giant of the canine race. It was to be seen in the halls of the Irish kings and as far as one can tell, its history goes back to the very earliest times. It was used, as its name shows, to hunt the wolves which caused great damage in Old Ireland.

BIG CATS . . .

The cat family is also a very large one. At one end of the scale are the lions and **tigers,** at the other is the cuddly little puss that purrs before your fire. In between there are a number of exciting and often dangerous animals. One member of the feline family is the jaguar, found mainly in South America. Next in size to the jaguar is the puma, sometimes called the mountain lion or cougar. Another cat, a little smaller still, is the leopard which lives in Africa and Asia. Another American 'big cat' is the ocelot, found between Texas and Patagonia. Then there are the lynx, snow leopard and jaguarondi, and also smaller wild cats which seem harmless but can be quite savage. These include the Persian lynx and the African caracal both very active and very fierce. What a family!

. . . AND LITTLE CATS

The ancient Egyptians were the first to tame cats. They did this so that they could be used to guard their grain stores against mice. This was about 4,000 years ago. They thought so much of these cats that when they died they were embalmed and buried like people. From Egypt, cats began to spread wherever there was civilization. At that time Europe was over-run with wild cats but in time most were destroyed, and now the great majority of cats in Europe are the domestic cats we know and love.

75

Animals swift and slow

In the animal kingdom, some creatures travel swiftly, others very slowly indeed. Of all animals, the cheetah is considered the fastest whilst the slowest mammal is the sloth, found in South America. It travels at an average speed of 0.157km/h (0.098mph). As slow as a snail, however, is right, for the common garden snail rarely moves faster than 0.05km/h (0.03mph).

CHEETAH

This beautiful creature is the fastest four-legged animal. One observer wrote: 'It can overtake upon open ground the well-known black buck, which surpasses in speed the highest bred greyhound.' Although a number of antelopes almost reach the **cheetah's** maximum speed, no other animal can accelerate faster. The cheetah differs from other big cats, having a small head but legs that are long and made for speed. It stands about 1m (3 feet) high and has a length of some 2.1m (7 feet). It has been used by man for centuries. It is captured then, when tamed, is trained to hunt antelope. Over short distances it can reach a speed of 70mph. When hunting, the cheetah's eyes are covered with a hood until an antelope is spotted. When near enough, the huntsman slips the hood from the animal's eyes and it then dashes after its prey. When this is caught, the cheetah does not shake or tear it, but grips it with its strong teeth. The hood is then replaced and more game is sought.

IMPALA

The **impala** is one of the most graceful of all antelopes. It lives in the plains and thorny savannah of South and East Africa. It is a fairly large animal, being more than 1m (3 feet) high, reddish-brown in colour and with a white underside. The male impala is known at once by its horns which are gracefully curved, rather like a lyre. It is a grazer and nearly always found near water. It is a very sociable animal and for part of the year lives in very large herds, usually near lakes. During the rainy season these vast herds break up into small units, each led by a male impala and up to two dozen females. The males that are left over, when the mates have been chosen, form into bands of 50 or so 'bachelors'.

When around the lake or water-hole, young bucks stand nearby to act as look-outs, to warn the others if an enemy such as a lion or leopard appears. The whole herd then takes to flight. They use their leaps (which make them soar 3m (10 feet) into the air, covering about 9m (30 feet) at a time.

SLOTH

The sloth is one of the slowest of animals – indeed it hardly moves at all. There are two types of sloth, recognized by the number of toes they have on their hands and feet. One is the three-toed sloth, an animal that lives – often upside down – in the forests of tropical America. It has a shaggy coat which becomes greenish in colour due to vegetable growth upon it.

The **two-toed sloth** (or Hoffmann's sloth) also lives in South America and is somewhat larger than the other. It spends most of its life in trees, where it moves very slowly – yet it can swim very well. When the two-toed sloth is rolled up in sleep it looks more like a bundle of hay than a living animal. It lives on all kinds of fruit and leaves, pulling the branches towards its mouth with its claws and then picking off what it wants with its sharp teeth.

79

SNAIL

Of all slow moving creatures, the **snail** is the slowest. Shakespeare himself wrote of the schoolboy: 'Creeping like snail, unwillingly to school' and there is much in that. For a snail takes two weeks to cover a mile. Yet despite their slowness, they are very interesting creatures to study. Their eyes are on the end of two stalks, usually called horns, which they push out but quickly draw in again if danger approaches. It also has a kind of tongue which, under a microscope, can be seen to be covered with numerous backward-pointing teeth. Snails lay as many as 100 eggs but only a few live.

TORTOISE

Tortoises belong to an order which also includes turtles and terrapins. Most have strong body-armour, known as the 'carapace' into which, when threatened, they draw their head, limbs and tail. Tortoises belong mainly to the warm areas of the earth. Slow-moving, they are the same sort of reptiles as they were 200 million years ago, having changed very little in all that time. They have no teeth but tear their food apart with a horny bill. Amongst the wide variety of tortoises are the **giant tortoises** of Galapagos, some of which reach a length of over 1.5m (5 feet)!

FALCON

In Tudor times, the most popular sport was falconry. As the quarry pursued included almost all the wild birds, hares and so on, there was no shortage of game. Still today the **peregrine falcon** soars high in the sky and then, sighting its prey, swoops down at a speed of up to 290km/h (180mph), making it the fastest hunting bird. Few are left now but many people are trying to breed these magnificent birds.

Colouring and camouflage

Many members of the animal kingdom practise camouflage. This means that by taking on the colour and, in some cases, the shape of their surroundings, they can hide from their enemies or catch any unwary victim that may pass their hiding place. Some change colour to fit the seasons; stoats, for example, change from reddish-brown to white, as do the Arctic fox and the Arctic hare. This colour change is so that they do not stand out as brown blobs against a wintry white landscape—camouflage, in fact.

SNAKES

For the most part, snakes are masters of camouflage. This has been forced on them because they have many enemies – the mongoose, the secretary bird and in Britain, the hedgehog. But their greatest enemies are other snakes. Most of the time snakes such as the grass snake hide, using their colouring to disappear amid the long grass. One species, the hog-nosed snake of North America goes one better. When discovered it suddenly collapses and lies, seemingly lifeless, and its attacker goes away. A perfect example of camouflage is the **rhinoceros viper** whose colouring merges perfectly with the ground over which it travels.

GECKO

This is a strange animal for it has suction pads on its feet which allow it to run up a vertical wall or glass window and then, carrying on, travel upside down across the ceiling. Its spotty colouring makes it almost invisible, especially when it hides amongst the lichen at the base of trees. In any case, geckos are hardly ever seen by day although at night, when they hunt, their strange call of 'tik-tik' may be heard. The **leaf-tailed gecko** is shown here.

HERON

The heron is one of a large family of birds allied to the bitterns. There are many species within this group although only one, the common heron, breeds in Britain. Others, however, visit Britain from time to time, including the great white heron, the little white heron and the night heron. They are long-legged, wading birds, living in marshes and watery areas, feeding on creatures such as frogs and fish.

The **purple heron,** a smaller bird than some, is a master of camouflage. Despite its colour it manages to choose places – even muddy swamps as here, to merge with its background.

PTARMIGAN

The ptarmigan grows its own camouflage. In summer it is a mottled brown, a colour that blends with earth and trees. Then, as winter approaches, it sheds these brown feathers to become completely white. It also grows feathery 'snowshoes', for during the long winter months it lives amid the snow and ice of northern climates. Some of the family live all the year in Scotland, especially in the Cairngorms. The bird shown here is the **willow ptarmigan.** Hen ptarmigans often deceive their attackers. When their nests are threatened they pretend to be injured,

crawling along the ground and leading the enemy away from the precious eggs or chicks.

BITTERN

For the most part, the **bittern** lives amongst the reeds on river banks and uses them as a perfect form of camouflage. If the bittern thinks that danger is near, it will 'freeze', with its neck and beak stretched straight up to the sky. Its neck and body feathers are also pressed hard against its body so that they blend with the reeds. Its streaked plumage matches its surroundings perfectly. This action helps it to escape its enemies looking for a meal, and it also helps it to get closer to its own prey.

SAND GROUSE

Although it is called a **sand grouse,** this bird is more closely related to the pigeon family. It lives in hot, desert places usually miles from the nearest water. Yet it knows that its chicks need water to live so it flies across the desert to the nearest pond or lake, soaks its feathers with water, then flies back to its nest where the chicks suck the water from the sodden feathers. Its plumage matches the sandy desert and when on the ground, it seems to disappear from sight.

85

CHAMELEON

Nature has arranged that this little reptile, a weak, almost defenceless creature, can hide itself by changing colour. There are some 50 types of chameleon; the most common being found on the African and Asian costs of the Mediterranean.

The one in the picture is a **Cape chameleon.** At night it is usually a whitish yellow, but as the day dawns it changes to a darkish green, like the leaves among which it lives. As the day goes on, the chameleon gets brighter and brighter. You may also watch it change colour to match new surroundings. It cannot change colour quite as much as some people in the past have believed, but it can change the strength of its colour and the variations in the pattern on its skin very quickly. Its changes seem to be caused mainly by the movement of sunlight through leaves. The chameleon also uses its camouflage for attack as well as defence – its prey is much less likely to see it if it blends into the background, and it can then use its swift tongue to catch the insect it is after.

FROG

Frogs belong to the amphibian family, which means that they can breathe under water through their skins as well as on dry land with their lungs, like other land-dwelling animals.

Most species of frog have very long back legs. These enable them to make their enormous jumps when danger threatens.

Frogs rarely wander far away from water and even the tree frogs who look for their food mainly among the leaves of small trees and shrubs prefer to stay fairly near water. This little **tree frog** shows what clever camouflage some frogs have. It is almost invisible against the branch on which it is sitting. The marks on its body are very similar indeed to those on the tree bark. This particular type of frog is different from all the others because it does not like rain and goes into hiding whenever the weather is wet! It makes a special large foam nest for its eggs to hatch out in. It is hung above a pond or stream so that when the eggs hatch, the baby tadpoles drop into the water below.

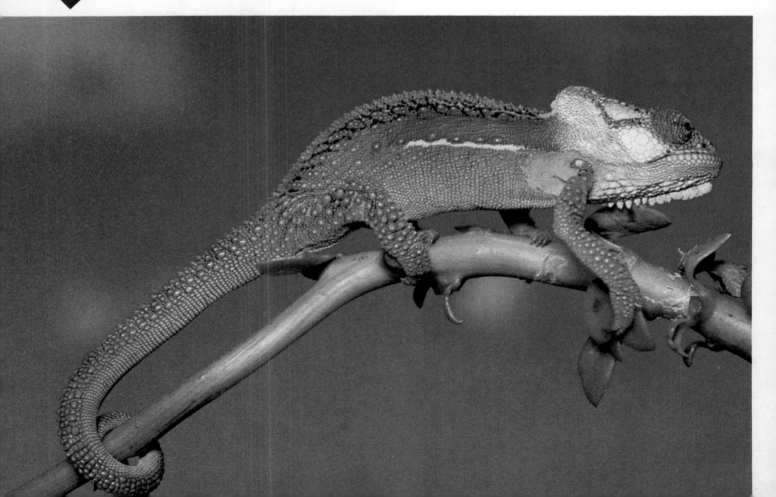

GROUND HOPPER

The insects which are called **ground hopper** are different from others of their family of grasshoppers and locusts, for they have a hood which stretches over almost their entire body. This hood plays an important part in their own special camouflage for their lives are spent in dry, stony places in South Africa and they use it to make them look exactly like the stones amongst which they live. Even the ground hopper's eyes and antennae are stone coloured so that they are almost impossible to pick out from their surroundings. Those that live in the tropics, especially those of South Africa, are very strange-looking. Some even have 'thorns' on their bodies so that they seem even more like the shrubby branch on which they happen to be clinging.

Another, found almost everywhere in the British Isles, is the common ground hopper. It lives on boggy moors and near marshes. Although it cannot fly it swims very well and can also manage to do very good leaps. ▶

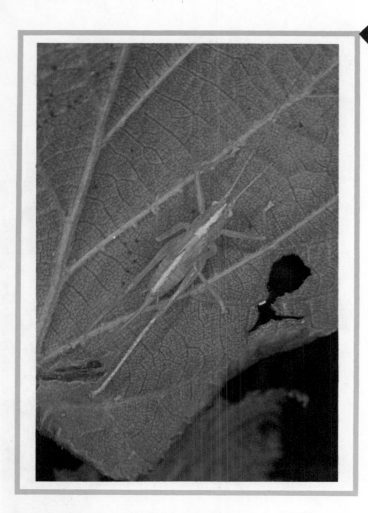

OAK BUSH CRICKET

This insect makes its home in oak trees because its colouring exactly matches those trees. It hides behind the leaves all during the day and only comes out at night to find food. The females lay their eggs in cracks in the bark and these hatch out during July. Crickets look very much like grasshoppers and, like them, make a 'song' by rubbing one hind leg on a leaf.

LEAF INSECT

Of all the disguises in nature, that of the **leaf insect** is one of the most remarkable. Some of them look like green leaves of plants, others like rough brown leaves; but they always match their surroundings perfectly. One group even has extra pieces on their legs which look like partly eaten leaves. All of them resemble leaves so closely that they can only be seen when their flat, thin bodies actually move.

88

SWALLOW-TAIL BUTTERFLY

Amongst the swallow-tail butterfly family are the largest and most brightly coloured of all butterflies. One, the **spicebush swallowtail,** uses camouflage to protect its young, its **caterpillar** having a large pair of eye markings on its body which frightens off other insects and birds.

MARSH BUTTERFLY

Another butterfly with 'eyes' to protect itself is the **marsh butterfly** found mainly in Africa. It is sometimes attacked by a bird which strikes for these same hairy eyes. When the attacker realises it is not a tasty little animal it usually flies off, leaving the marsh butterfly damaged, but still alive.

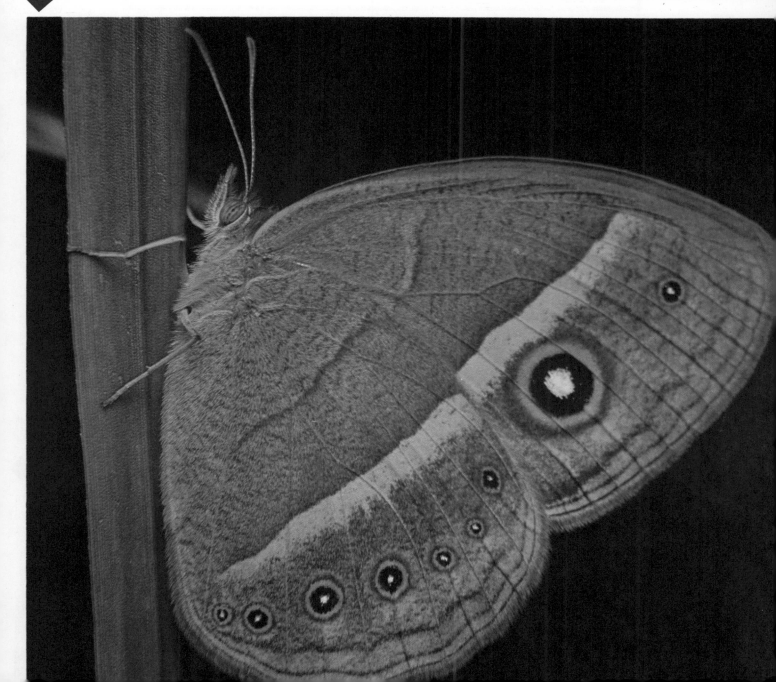

GEOFFROYS MARMOSET

The marmosets are the most attractive of all the monkeys and amongst the smallest of the group known as the primates. The **Geoffroys marmoset** is a pretty little creature and, as can be seen, is about the size of a squirrel and with a coat that perfectly matches the trees it lives in.

BABOON

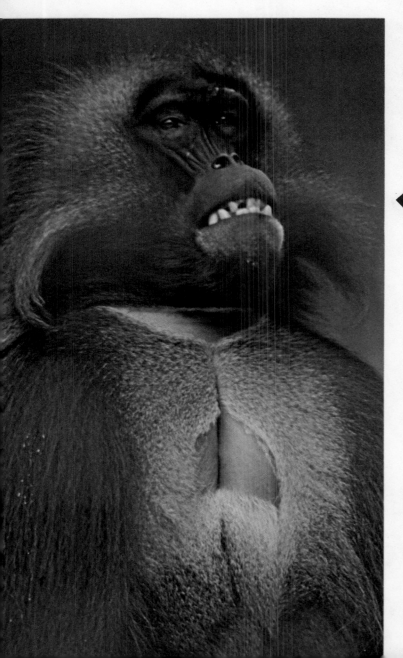

Of all the monkey tribe, none are more brutal or ferocious than the **baboons,** large African apes about 1m (3 feet) high. They are also masters of camouflage, their greyish skin blending with the trees from which they emerge, often in very large numbers, to do great damage to plantations and crops. Despite their fierce temper, however, they can be tamed to become a favourite in zoos.

GOLDEN MARMOSET

The magnificent mane of shimmering golden-orange worn by this marmoset makes it easily spotted by eagles and other enemies. Because of this it lives mainly in the forests of Brazil where it travels from tree to tree at great speed.

ZEBRA

The most brightly camouflaged of all animals is surely the **zebra.** Someone once described it as a horse wearing a football jersey! Basically, its colour is white upon which is laid a series of glossy, jet-black stripes, which cover it from head to tail except for its underparts. It is a member of the *Equidae,* as the horse family is known, and there are three main species—the mountain zebra, common zebra and Grévy's zebra. All have the same unusual markings although they live in different places. Of the three, the common zebra is the one whose markings change quite a lot, as the farther north one goes the more

vivid the stripes become. Grévy's zebra is the largest of the three yet has the narrowest stripes. Their arrangement is most attractive.

It is very difficult to get near to a zebra because, when the herd is feeding, sentries are posted to give the alarm if any danger is near. At a signal, the whole herd are off like the wind, usually to lose themselves among any trees or nearby scrub where, standing quite still, they become almost invisible. Even so, if flight is not possible, they can still defend themselves very well. The males join in a tight circle, with their heads together, and lash out at their attackers with their hind hooves.

DEER

It is easy to confuse deer with members of a different family—the antelopes. The main difference is in their antlers. Deer have solid antlers which fall off and grow again each year, whilst the antelopes have solid horns which stay on all their lives. Within the deer family there is a great difference in size—from the giant moose of North America which reaches 2.1m (7 feet) in height to the tiny deer of South America and Asia, little more than 30cm (12in) high. At one time Britain contained thousands of deer, but as the forests were cut down, many were killed off. Today a fairly common deer in Britain is the **roe deer** which is to be found in some parts of England and almost all over Scotland. It is the smallest native species in Europe, even an adult buck (male deer) being little more than 60cm (2 feet) high. Its antlers are shed in November and grow again by the following February. Although these antlers rarely grow more than 30cm (12 in) long, the deer have been known to kill a man with them. Yet this is rare, for the roe deer is a shy and timid creature which lives most often in the heart of a forest or wood with its family.

Like many other animals its colour changes according to the season—dark reddish-brown in summer, and grey with a tinge of yellow, in winter. When the roe deer is hunted it often escapes capture by a number of clever tricks. It never runs in a straight line but doubles back on its former track so that the pursuing hounds become very confused. Then, with a sudden spring, it will leap behind a bush and as it lies quite still, the hounds often pass it without knowing they are near their quarry.

SARDINES

These small fish, which most people only think of as a tasty snack in a tin, are very cleverly camouflaged. The markings fit its way of life which is to come up to the surface, only at night, to feed. Its camouflage lies in the way the body is shaded. Its back is dark green, its sides a golden colour and its underside silver. This means that when looked down on from above, the darkish top matches the surrounding water; when looked up at from below by a possible enemy, its light underside blends with the sky above. **Sardines** often swim in very dense shoals and this gives them protection against attackers.

They are fished at night by men using nets. They live mainly in the Mediterranean, along the coasts of Italy and Sardinia.

EELS

These are fishes with long, snake-like bodies. The common European eel lives in fresh water lakes and rivers yet travels from its home to the sea. Reaching the sea, it sets off on the long journey to the Atlantic Ocean where the young eels, known as elvers, are born. Later these elvers set out on the return trip to fresh water once more. Some eels, however, are already living in tropical waters. These are the **moray eels** which, from their clever camouflage, are also called Painted Eels. Here is one against a background which it matches.

WOBBEGONG SHARK

Not all sharks have that slim, streamlined look we usually expect of this fish. One, the **Wobbegong** or **Carpet Shark,** is quite different. It has a broad, flat head and a blunt snout, whilst the sides of its head have heavy tassels of skin. It has a very wide mouth which contains slim, pointed teeth. At first glance it looks nothing like a shark at all. There are three species of this fish, mainly found off the coasts of Japan, China and Australia. Its skin is of a strange, mottled colour which blends perfectly into the coral on which it rests, looking exactly like a rock overgrown with seaweed. Its shape makes it impossible to go swiftly in pursuit of its prey like other sharks. Instead it relies on cunning. It lies perfectly still on coral, rocks or weeds on the sea bed until a fish or a crustacean comes along within reach of its powerful jaws. The largest of the three species can be anything up to 3.2m (10ft 6in) long. They are harmless to man unless attacked, when they will give a fierce bite.

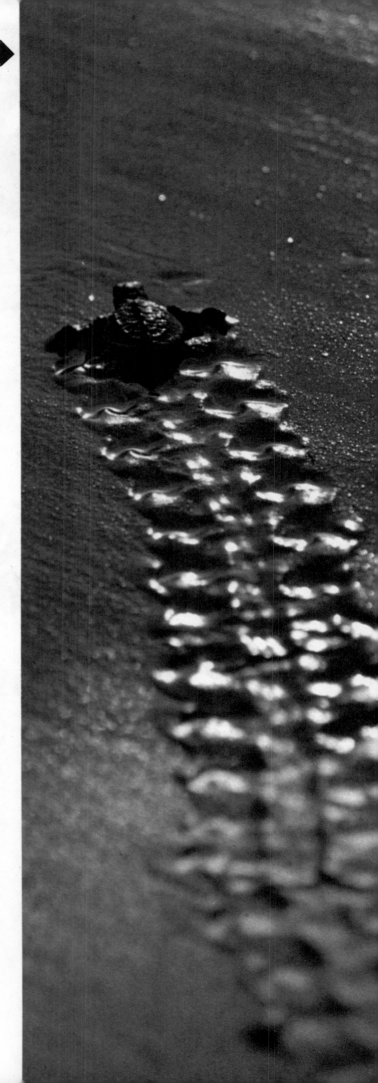

BABY TURTLE

A newly-hatched baby marine turtle, scuttling down to the beach towards the safety of the sea.

Through the pages of this book we have taken a journey through Nature's wonderland. We have read of the mighty whales, the largest creatures that have ever lived, existing on the tiny life form known as plankton; how that ungainly bird, the ostrich, has never enjoyed flying like its other featured friends; how the sleek, striped tiger stalks its prey through the half-light of the Indian jungle . . . and so much more of this wonderful world of nature.

Yet we must be on our guard that, in years to come, these fascinating creatures will still be living on this marvellous world. Already over 800 different kinds of animal life – elephants, tigers, and hundreds of different types of birds and fishes – are all threatened with extinction. All of us must try and save as much as possible of this colourful world, for those who come after us to enjoy as well.

Acknowledgments

The publishers would like to thank the following individuals and organizations for their kind permission to reproduce the photographs in this book:

Ardea 31 above, (K W Fink) 35 above, 46, 47, 59 above, 66, 90 below, (P Steyn) 58 left, (R & V Taylor) 20, (W Weisser) 55 below, (J S Wightman) 56-57, 76-77, 85 left; A.F.A. Colour Library 59 below; Heather Angel 10, 16-17, 27; Douglass Baglin 32-33; V Baldwin 37; Barnaby's Picture Library 75 above; Bavaria Verlag 80 below; G B Blossom 82; Ron Boardman 64; British Museum (Imitor) 6, 8, (C M Dixon) 9; F Bruemmer 24, 26 above; Camera Press Ltd. 34; Bruce Coleman Ltd. 31 below, 41, 48 centre, (D & J Bartlett) 60, (Jane Burton) endpapers, 15 above, 61, 84 left, 85 right, 88 above and below, 92, 93, (Jeff Foott) 32, (Lee Lyon) 67, (J Markham) 4, (H Maynard) 96, (D A J Mobbs) 30 above, (C Old) 84 right, (H Reinhard) 62-63, (Stouffer Productions) 2-3; Ben Cropp 68 above; A Cumbers 36, 38 below; P M David 14; Euro Colour Library 7 left; S Halliday 74 above; Jacana Agence de Presse (J L S Dubois) 18, (M Kalifa) 28, (G Munschy,) 23 below; P Johnson 83; A B Klots 89 above; Frank Lane 23 above, 29 left, 58 right, (N Duerden) 81; Claire Leimbach 65; J Marchington 54; Moorfield Aquatics 11, 13; N.H.P.A. 74 below, (A Anderson) 50, (A Bannister) 42, 43 left and right, 45, 86, 87 above and below, 89 below, (Bruce Barnetson) 15 below, (F Blackburn) 48 below, (J Blossom) 57, (S Dalton) 44 above, 51 below, 52 below, (F Erize) 90 above, (B Hawkes) 49 above, 51 above, (P Johnson) 25, 53, (K B Newman) 40, 52 above, 56 above, (L Perkins) 44 below, (A G Wells) 56 below, (L B Williamson) 80 above; Natural Science Photos 7 right, 35 below; Photo Aquatics (Herman Gruhl) 19 below, 94 above, (R Lubbock) 94 below; Pictor International (FPG-J Baker) 22 right; Picture-point Ltd. 49 below; B Risden 55 above; San Diego Zoo 91; Sea Library (Ken Balcomb) 68 below, (Carl Roessler) 16 left, 19 above; Seaphot (B Cropp) 95, (P M David) 69, (Christian Petron) 21 left, (Flip Schulke) 21 right; Spectrum Colour Library 72, 73 below; S A Thompson 1, 38 above, 70, 71; Tony Stone Associates (Ron Church) 22 left, 26 below; ZEFA 73 above, (J Grossauer) 39, 75 below.